Expose

Chey Lushman

Presentation by *BookLeaf Publishing*

Web: www.bookleafpub.com

E-mail: info@bookleafpub.com

ISBN: 9789395756983

First edition 2022

DEDICATION

I want to dedicate this to anyone who has been lost, or hurt. There's hope, and it does get better.

ACKNOWLEDGEMENT

I'd like to thank my friend Adrianna Park for sending me the link to this challenge, and my friend Brittany Sheppard for always encouraging me and being the biggest fan of my poetry. I'd also like to thank my siblings for just bringing me so much joy. Without you all this would have still been a pipe dream.

PREFACE

Some of these poems are a few years old, and some I wrote specifically for this book. Poetry has gotten me through all of my feelings when spoken words wouldn't quite come out. I hope it helps to encourage its readers.

WARNING: Some topics in this may be triggering for some people. It deals with abuse, mental health, trauma, and overcoming them.

French Kiss

Next time I'll bite my tounge
And hope you're there
To kiss away the blood.

Blossoming

I have handpicked this feeling.
I hold it now
Like the precious bouquet it is.
Offering you one of
The delicate blossoms
Hoping you will treat it as it deserves.

Creation

Ink stained hands
Where I have
Written myself
Into existence.

Thank you (sis)

Justice for all that could have been
Is in this gift.
So simple. So pure.
Proof that despite it all, you're still
on my side. That we're still together.
That we can be better
Than anyone ever expected us to be.

Cherry Heart

May one of the world's comforts
Be yours.
For you, my Cherry Heart.

My Cherry Heart kisses me
So sweetly
That for a moment
I, too am made of sugar.

The sugar on my lips dissolves. It leaves a bitter
taste behind.
And yet I still wait for a bite to
Return to the sweetness of before.

Why must I crave your sweetness? When I know
deep down,
It is the poison you use to
End me.
(I will gladly let you take my life)

Failure

I try
I fail
I give up.

I try
I fail
I give up.

The circle seems never ending. A constant swirl
of anguish.

Each failure makes me more jaded.
Each time I give up it's harder to start again.

But I try
I try
I try.

Contradiction

Say the waves are mountains.
Caress my ears with your lies.
Tell me I'm
Bad
Beaten
Broken.

Lather your traps in honey
And look me in the eyes.
Tell me I'm worthy.
Tell me I'm worthless.

Go back and forth
With your loving
And your hating.

Tell me this is all to heal me,
When really you're trying to
Break
Me
Apart.

Incredible

Suffering in silence
With your promises
Tumbling into my own insecurities.

Another 'one that got away'.
I don't know if I'm pissed or heartbroken.

"Had things been different"
Feels like a cruel joke.

Heritability

You are starting to falter
And I am starting to fight.

In slow, steady increments.
I am lashing at you with your own tounge,

And you are bleeding from my wounds.
You counter attack like a wounded animal,

Alone. And afraid.
How I was for so long under your thumb.

You are slowly being beaten down,
No longer the monster from my memories.

I will fear you no longer
It's your time
To fear me.

On Healing

Discard of me
Before you're done.
Leave me to be ruined.
Let me rip you open
Just a bit.
Tearing at your skin
As you tear at mine.
Both of us being destroyed and coming back
together.

Recipe for disaster

1 cup of too much sleep, stir in a teaspoon of
yawns.
A half cup of groggy mindlessness
And 3/4th of frustration.

Mix all together and cook at 350°c
Should be a nice mixture of blue and black.
If needed, add tears and fears to taste.

And there you have it! The perfect recipe for
personal disaster

Mom

Call your mother to feel better or worse. The ache you feel fills you either way with a sad sort of love.

Iridescent

The rain twines
Around your coloured hair
Making the usual silky locks
Iridescent as fireworks.

Lies as Sweet as Summer

There is a sun burning in me,
Its scorching my skin
Trying to escape my chest,
But I
Swallow
It
Down
With a glass of salt water
And tell the world I'm fine.

Demise

So sorry that you
are missing out on
Everything I am
And everything I will be.
Your neggelince has led to this.
My growth
From your demise.

Homemade Happy Ending

Tragedy etched into bones,
skin stretched thin
Across old scars.
I reach through them all
And pull out my
Happy ending.

Him

Careful
He
Expects
you
To be somehow more and less
Of who you really are.

Forget about me

Forget all you
Know about me.
I have torn it up and fed
It to the ocean.
It has long since
 been swallowed up
By sea foam and all that's left
Is all the things you refuse to see.

Are you with me?

Are you with me?
Can you understand
Where I'm coming from?
I ache to know
If you feel the same.

Speak

Talk to me.
Give me the inspiration I need.
Slow and soft,
I'm fragile y'know.

For you

Attention,
Earth to you,
You are so beautiful
And so strong.
You've come so far
And you'll keep going.